Things I Can Do

There are many things I can do
Maybe you can do them too;

I know how to climb a tree
I can even buzz like a bee,
I can also wash my face
And I know how to run a race.
I know how to talk to a dog
I can even croak like a frog,
I can also sail a boat
And I know how to sink not float.

I know how to build a house
I can even be still as a mouse,
I can also kick a ball
And I know how to never fall.

I know how to tame a bear
I can even comb my hair,
I can also catch a snake
And I know how to stay awake.

There are many more things I can do
Tomorrow I'll teach them all to you.

B. Taylor Bradford

Little People™ Big Book

About
OURSELVES

ALEXANDRIA, VIRGINIA

Table of Contents

Me Myself

My Body

My Feelings

My Day

As We Grow

Me
Myself

Me I Am!

I am the only ME I AM
who qualifies as me;
no ME I AM has been before,
and none will ever be.

No other ME I AM can feel
the feelings I've within;
no other ME I AM can fit
precisely in my skin.

There is no other ME I AM
who thinks the thoughts I do;
the world contains one ME I AM,
there is no room for two.

I am the only ME I AM
this earth shall ever see;
that ME I AM I always am
is no one else but ME!

Jack Prelutsky

ALL ABOUT ME

This is all about you! Read the sentences and point to the pictures that tell what's true about you.

This is a story about me.

I am a

I live in a

When we go visiting, I like to travel by

When I wake up in the morning, the first thing I do is

6

If I could have any pet I wanted,
I would have a

When I feel sad, I

When I feel happy, I

When I grow up, I might want to be a

7

When it rains, I wear a

In the summer, I like to go to the

When it snows, I wear a

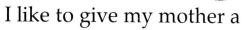

I like to give my mother a

The Bear Who Wanted to Be a Bird

by Adele and Cateau De Leeuw

There once was a little black bear who wanted to be a bird. He wished it so hard, and thought about it so much, that finally he decided he was one.

Going through the forest one day, he saw some birds high up in a tree. "Hello," he said. "I'm a bird, too."

The birds laughed at him. "*You're* not a bird," they said. "Birds have beaks."

The little black bear scurried through the forest until he found a thin piece of wood that had a point. He tied it to his muzzle and hurried back to the tree where the birds sat. "See," he cried, looking up, "I have a beak!"

"Just the same," they said, "you're not a bird. Birds have feathers."

So the little black bear ran as fast as he could out of the forest and found a chicken yard. There were lots of feathers lying on the ground. He picked them up and went back to the forest. There he sat down on some pine needles and stuck the feathers all over his head and his shoulders and down his front legs. Then he went to the tree where the birds sat and cried happily, "I have feathers, too. See, I'm a bird."

But the birds only laughed at him. "*You're* not a bird," they said. "Don't you know that birds sing?"

The little black bear felt sad, but not for long. He remembered that deep in the forest was a house where a singing teacher lived. He went there and knocked on the door. "Please teach me to sing," he begged. "I must learn to sing."

"It's most unusual," said the singing teacher, "but I will try. I have a wonderful system. Come in. Open your mouth. Now follow me – *do, re, mi, re, do . . . do, re, mi, re, do.*"

The little black bear practiced and practiced and practiced for a whole week, and then, feeling that he was very good indeed, he hurried back to the tree where the birds were.

"Listen," he cried. "I can sing, too." And he opened his mouth very wide, and in a deep voice sang, "*Do, re, mi, re, do . . . do, re, mi, re, do.*"

The birds laughed harder than ever. "You're not a bird," they told him. "Birds fly."

The little black bear said, "I can fly, too." He lifted first one foot, all covered with feathers, and then the other, and then hopped up and down, lifting both together. But he did not fly.

"I must get higher off the ground," he said. "Watch me." So he went to a big rock nearby and climbed up on it, and looked over the edge. The ground seemed very far away. "But," he thought, "maybe if I take a running start, and don't look down, it will be all right." So he backed off, closed his eyes, ran as fast as he could to the edge of the rock, lifted his feet, flapped them – and fell, with a loud smack, on his little behind on the ground.

He opened his eyes, and felt the tears coming. It hurt where he had fallen. His beak had slipped off; feathers were lying all over the ground.

The little birds laughed and laughed, high up in the tree, and then they all flew away together.

"You're not a bird," they called, and their words floated back to him on the wind. "You're not a bird, you're a bear."

He picked himself up and walked slowly through the forest. He felt very bad, and everything ached.

He rubbed his muzzle, and was glad that the clumsy beak wasn't tied to it anymore. He picked the rest of the feathers off himself, and his fur felt soft and furry. He found a bush with some beautiful red berries on it. They looked good, and he went over and stripped some off and ate them. They were delicious – much, much nicer than the worms that birds had to eat – and he ran his tongue around his black muzzle and pulled off another bunch.

After a while he met another bear, just about his size, coming toward him in the forest. "Hello," said the other bear.

"Wuf, wuf," said the little black bear. And he thought, "I like the sound of that. It's much better than having to sing *do, re, mi, re, do* in a deep voice."

"Come and see what I've found," his new friend said.

He led him to a big tree and climbed it. "Follow me," he said, and the little black bear did. Up in the first limb was a bee's nest and a big comb of honey.

"Oh," said the little black bear, "what a wonderful find!" He dipped his paw in and licked it.

"I'm *glad* I'm a bear," he said. "Who would want to be a bird, anyhow?"

12

IF

What would it be like to be an animal? Try this game and see!

If I were a horse,
I'd neigh, of course!
(Hold two fingers up on either side of head and make neighing sounds.)

If I were a hen,
I'd scratch in my pen!
(Flap arms and pretend to scratch ground with feet.)

If I were a snail,
I'd crawl on the trail!
(Raise hands over head in roof shape. Bend forward a little and make crawling motion with fingers.)

If I were a bug,
I'd curl up in a rug!
(Cup hands, then hug self.)

If I were a pig,
I'd dance a jig!
(Puff cheeks out to look piggish and hop from foot to foot.)

But since I'm me,
I'll laugh, "Hee hee!"
(Hold belly and laugh.)

13

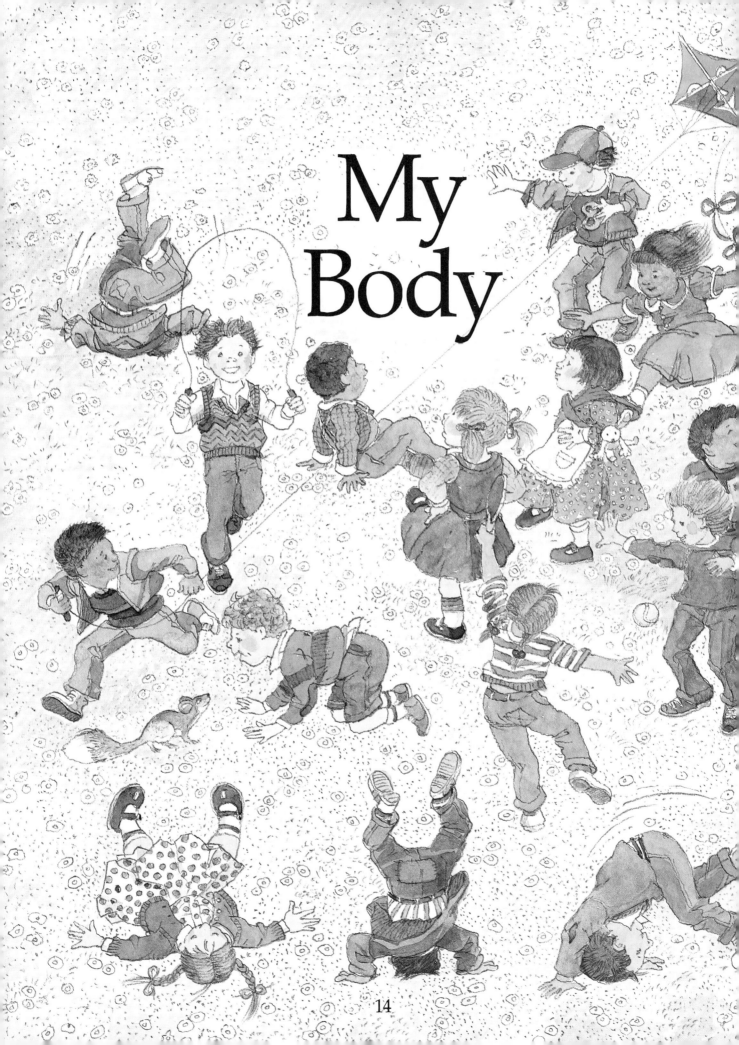

My Body

Somersaults

It's fun turning somersaults
and bouncing on the bed,
I walk on my hands
and I stand on my head.

I swing like a monkey
and I tumble and I shake,
I stretch and I bend,
but I never never break.

I wiggle like a worm
and I wriggle like an eel,
I hop like a rabbit
and I flop like a seal.

I leap like a frog
and I jump like a flea,
there must be rubber
inside of me.

Jack Prelutsky

OUR BODIES

What parts of your body can you find on a clock?
A face and two hands!

Read these silly riddles. After you read each riddle, look at the picture. Which part of the body is the riddle about? Point to that part of the body on the picture.

What is the last thing you should take off each night before you go to bed?
   You should take your feet off the floor!

What kind of bird is in your throat?
   The swallow!

What part of your face is like a skunk?
   Your nose – because it smells!

What animals do you have on your legs?
   Your calves!

Should you jump around on an empty stomach?
   No! You should jump around on your feet!

Why is your hair like a baby goose?
   Because it grows down!

What part of your body do you overlook when you read a book?
   Your nose!

What flowers do you have on your face?
   Two lips (Tulips)!

On which side of your body do you have the most skin?
   The outside!

Big Feet Are Neat, Sometimes

by Laura Hitchcock

Two towns away, and not so long ago, there lived a boy named Chester Wellington, who loved sports. No matter what the game—kickball, tag, or hide-and-seek—Chester Wellington always wanted to play.

Trouble was, the other kids didn't want to play with Chester. That's because Chester had a big problem. Or rather, he had two big problems—namely, two of the largest, most gigantic feet any of the kids had ever seen! He was always tripping over his own feet. And so were all the other kids.

The kids tried letting Chester play hide-and-seek. But wherever he hid, his feet always peeked out. Under a bush, behind a stone wall, or up in a tree, Chester was always found immediately.

They tried letting him play tag. But when Chester started running, he couldn't help thinking about his feet. "Flap-flap-flap!" they went against the ground. And when he thought about his feet . . . he tripped. Racing up behind him, Belinda Bradley also tripped. Then "Bebop" Harris, Marty Clinker, Roberta Woo, too, . . . until everyone in the neighborhood was sitting—BOOM!—on their rear ends. Belinda Bradley yelled, "Frog-feet! Chester's got frog-feet!"

That's how big Chester's feet were.

"Stay hopeful!" Chester's mother advised. "Unexpected things do happen!"

But Chester didn't feel hopeful. His feet grew so quickly, he had to buy new shoes twice as often as anybody else. Even the shoe salesman said, "Whoo-ee! What a pair of whoppers!"

"But," said Chester, "there must be other kids with feet this big!"

"Nope," said the salesman. "Not a chance."

Chester sighed. A game of kickball was scheduled for the very next Saturday—and Chester really wanted to play. But how? When he'd asked Belinda if he could play, she'd just giggled. Under her breath, she'd added, "Rib-bit! Rib-bit!" Everyone laughed. Poor Chester Wellington.

He had to do something! So, he did foot exercises. He wiggled his toes. He jumped up and down. He rocked, heel-to-toe, eighty times a day.

On the day of the game, Chester walked to the playground as usual. At least he could watch, he thought. If Belinda laughed . . . well, he would just ignore her.

But there was no laughter during the game. The other team was mean, and the game was very close. Then, when the game was almost over, Roberta felt sick and couldn't play any longer. There was only one thing to do—bring in Chester Wellington!

Belinda and the others tried not to look discouraged as Chester joined them. They couldn't help groaning when they realized Chester was up next! The score was five to five. It was the end of the game. Chester was their only hope!

As the ball raced toward him, Chester gathered his courage. "I will not trip!" he whispered to himself. He ran at the ball and kicked with all his might.

For a moment, he was afraid to look where the ball had gone. Then he forgot his fear because his entire team was screaming, "RU-U-UN!"

Chester didn't wait to be told again—he ran! "Flap-flap-flap!" went his big feet, as he sped around the bases. But he didn't trip!

The other players threw the ball from outfield to infield. Some ran toward Chester, desperately hoping to catch the ball and tag him out.

But none of them had ever played against someone with feet as large as Chester's. BOOM! BOOM! BOOM! Down they all went, tripping and falling, trying to avoid Chester's gigantic feet. The ball bounced away, beyond the sidelines.

Chester flew across home plate. All the kids cheered, even Belinda! He had made the winning run.

After that game, the other kids let Chester play kickball more and more often. Before long, he was the best kickball player in the neighborhood, in spite of his huge feet.

But then another unexpected thing happened. Chester began to grow, and grow . . . and grow! After a while, his feet no longer looked gigantic—mainly because they finally fit the rest of his body! And as he grew strong and tall, he also became the best athlete in the state. Professional teams from all over the country begged him to play for them. At last, Chester Wellington could play any sport he wanted.

But . . . Chester decided not to become a professional athlete, after all. Instead, he became a tap dancer. He traveled the world, dancing, and he always sent funny postcards to his friends back home.

Of course, it was all quite unexpected. But that's the way things happen!

Ears Hear

Flies buzz,
Motors roar.
Kettles hiss,
People snore.
Dogs bark,
Birds cheep.
Autos honk: *Beep! Beep!*

Winds sigh,
Shoes squeak.
Trucks honk,
Floors creak.
Whistles toot,
Bells clang.
Doors slam: *Bang! Bang!*

Kids shout,
Clocks ding.
Babies cry,
Phones ring.
Balls bounce,
Spoons drop.
People scream: *Stop! Stop!*

Lucia and James L. Hymes, Jr.

22

Ears **hear,** eyes **see,** noses **smell,** mouths **taste,** hands **touch.**

Use your **eyes** to **see** pictures of all the things that make sounds in the poem.

Now take another look. Can you find things in this picture that you **taste** with your **mouth**?

Can you find things that **smell** good when you smell them with your **nose?**

Can you find things that are nice to **touch** with your **hands**?

23

DID YOU EVER WONDER
ABOUT THE BODY

Why do I get hiccups?
You get hiccups when a muscle in your body called the diaphragm gets a shock. Your diaphragm is a muscle under your ribs that moves up and down to help you breathe. Hiccups happen when the diaphragm moves up and down too fast. This can happen when you gulp in air – for example, when you're laughing, crying, or eating too fast.

Why does my stomach growl?
When you eat, you swallow air along with your food. Your stomach moves around as it digests your food. When there's no food left, it moves the air around. This makes growling noises.

Why do I blink?

You blink to keep your eyes clean and healthy. Inside each eye, you have a tear gland. Tear glands make tears to keep your eyes clean. Every time you blink, tears spread over your eyes. They wash off dirt and keep your eyes from getting too dry.

Why am I ticklish?

You have nerve endings underneath your skin. Some are very sensitive. When someone touches you in a sensitive spot, the nerve endings send a message to your brain. This makes you giggle.

Why do I shiver when I'm cold?

When you're cold, it means your body's heat, or temperature, has gone down. Your muscles then shiver to make heat. Shivering warms your body.

TAP AND CLAP

To tap and clap and stomp and romp, just say these rhymes and follow the instructions.

Can You Walk On Tiptoe?

Can you walk on tiptoe,
As softly as a cat?

(Walk on tiptoe.)

And can you stamp along
the road
Stamp, stamp, just like that?

(Stamp your feet.)

Can you take some great big
strides
Just like a giant can?

(Walk with giant steps.)

Or walk along so slowly
Like a little old man?

(Walk bent over, with tiny, slow steps.)

Clap Your Hands

Clap your hands,
clap your hands
Clap them just like me.

Tap your knees,
tap your knees,
Tap them just like me.

Touch your shoulders,
touch your shoulders,
Touch them just like me.

Shake your head,
shake your head,
Shake it just like me.

Clap your hands,
clap your hands,
Now let them quiet be.

(Action as indicated by pictures.)

Sneezles

Christopher Robin
Had wheezles
And sneezles,
They bundled him
Into
His bed.
They gave him what goes
With a cold in the nose,
And some more for a cold
In the head.
They wondered
If wheezles
Could turn
Into measles,
If sneezles
Would turn
into mumps;
They examined his chest
For a rash,
And the rest
Of his body for swellings and lumps.

They sent for some doctors
In sneezles
And wheezles
To tell them what ought
To be done.
All sorts and conditions
Of famous physicians
Came hurrying round
At a run.

They all made a note
Of the state of his throat,
They asked if he suffered from thirst;
They asked if the sneezles
Came after the wheezles,
Or if the first sneezle
Came first.
They said, "If you teazle
A sneezle
Or wheezle,
A measle
May easily grow.
But humor or pleazle
The wheezle
Or sneezle,
The measle
Will certainly go."

They expounded the reazles
For sneezles
And wheezles,
The manner of measles
When new.
They said "If he freezles
In draughts and in breezles,
Then PHTHEEZLES
May even ensue."

Christopher Robin
Got up in the morning,
The sneezles had vanished away.
And the look in his eye
Seemed to say to the sky,
"Now, how to amuse them to-day?"

A.A. Milne

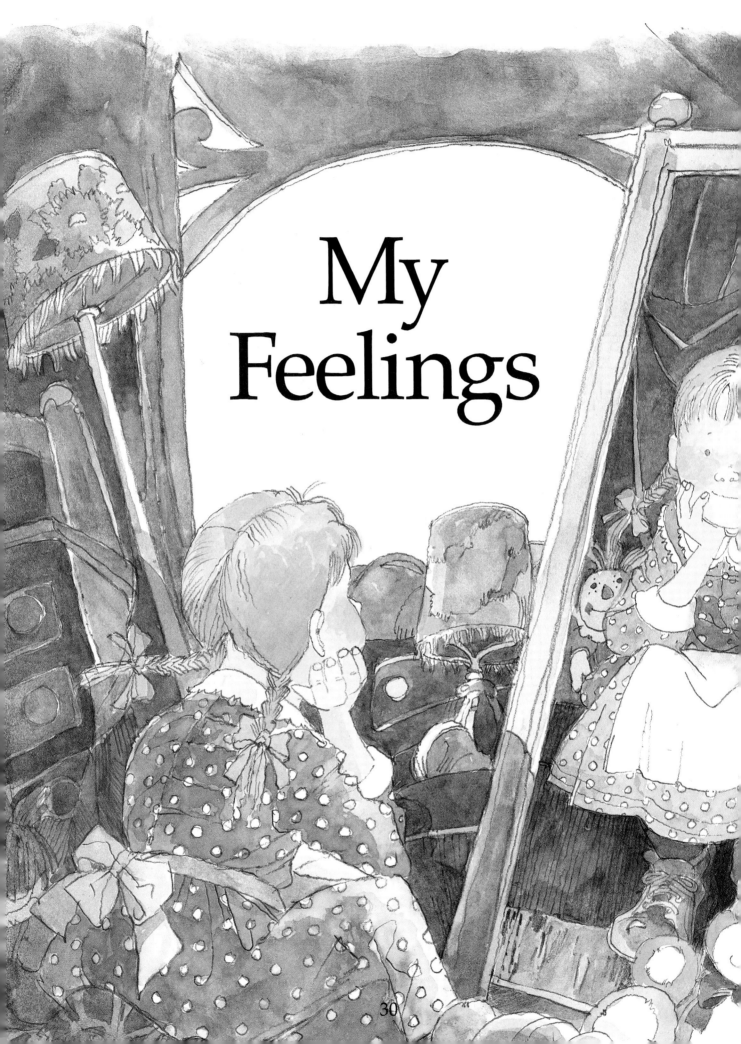

My Feelings

Changing

I know what I feel like;
I'd like to be *you*
And feel what *you* feel like
And do what *you* do.
I'd like to change places
For maybe a week
And look like your look-like
And speak as you speak
And think what you're thinking
And go where you go
And feel what you're feeling
And know what you know.
I wish we could do it;
What fun it would be
If I could try you out
And you could try me.

Mary Ann Hoberman

MOLLY AND MAXWELL ARE FRIENDS

Molly and Maxwell are best friends. They each have many different feelings. You have many different feelings, too. Do you ever feel like Molly and Maxwell?

When Molly feels silly, she makes funny faces. When Maxwell feels happy, he sings and dances.

Maxwell feels proud when he teaches Molly new words. Molly feels sad when her ice cream falls from its cone.

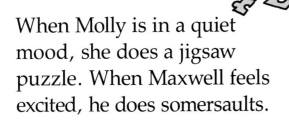

When Molly is in a quiet mood, she does a jigsaw puzzle. When Maxwell feels excited, he does somersaults.

Maxwell feels curious when he sees a butterfly in the yard. Molly feels shy when she meets someone for the first time.

When Molly feels angry, she stomps her feet. When Maxwell feels serious, he reads a book.

Sometimes, Molly feels bored because she has nothing to do. And Maxwell feels lonely because he has no one to play with. So, Molly and Maxwell play together.

And they both feel very special, because they're best friends.

The Frog Prince

*A Retelling of the Fairy Tale
by the Brothers Grimm*

nce there was a Princess who had a beautiful golden ball. It had been given to her when she was a little girl, and although she had long outgrown toys, she still liked to throw her ball high into the air and catch it. One bright morning, during a walk in the castle garden, she threw her ball high, but it fell into a well. It sank to the bottom before she could reach it.

The Princess sobbed, for she thought her ball was lost forever. She peered down into the dark well, but it was so deep she couldn't see the bottom. "Oh, I would give gold and jewels to anyone who could help me get my ball!" she cried.

At this, a frog poked his head out of the water and said, "Why are you sobbing, my friend?"

The Princess said, "Oh, frog, if you could toss my ball to me, I would give you anything you asked for!"

"Would you welcome me into your house, and let me eat from your plate?" asked the frog. "Would you let me sleep on your clean pillowcase?"

"I would surely welcome you into my house, and offer you food from my plate, and smooth the pillowcase for you to rest on, if only you would get my golden ball for me!"

The frog said, "Well, then, I'll do what I can if you promise to keep your word." He dived down into the water and soon reappeared with the golden ball balanced on his head. But as soon as the frog hopped to the edge of the well, the Princess snatched the golden ball, and with a cry of delight, she ran all the way back to the castle, leaving the frog behind.

That evening, the Princess was eating supper with the King and Queen when they heard a sound at the door, a kind of squishy knocking. "Who is it?" called the King.

"It is I, a humble frog," said a voice. "The Princess promised to welcome me into her home."

"Never!" yelled the Princess. "Nasty, ugly old frog!"

"My dear," said her father, "did you promise a frog he could come to call?"

"In exchange for finding her golden ball," called the frog from outside the door.

"Then, my dear, you must keep your word," said the King.

The King and Queen went and opened the door. In hopped the frog, looking around with interest. "Quite a nice castle," he said. "What's for supper?"

"You can't eat here!" yelled the Princess.

"But you promised me food from your plate," said the frog.

"My darling, if you promised," said the Queen, "you must keep your word. I insist."

"Have some food from my plate," said the Princess, in a voice that sounded rather rude. The frog jumped onto the table and sampled a bit of everything, and smacked his froggy lips.

"Now I'm tired," he said when he'd finished his meal. "It's time to be carried to your bed, so I may sleep on your pillowcase, just as you promised."

"I refuse! It cannot be!" shouted the Princess.

"If you promised, sweet daughter," said the King and Queen together, "you must keep your word."

The Princess shuddered with disgust, but she picked up the frog and carried him to her bedroom, where she set him down on the pillowcase. And he slept very comfortably all night long.

In the morning, he hopped away, but he returned in the evening for a second night, and again for a third. Each time the Princess kept her promise by opening the door to him, letting him eat from her plate and sleep on her pillow.

On the morning after the third night, the Princess opened her eyes to see that the frog was gone. But standing next to her bed was a handsome young man who said, "Good morning, Princess. I am a Prince who hopped to your side for the last three evenings as a humble frog. I have been freed from the spell cast upon me by a wicked witch because you kept your promise. It would give me the greatest pleasure if you would agree to be my wife, for I have grown to love and admire a Princess who keeps her word, even to a lowly frog."

The startled Princess ran to tell her parents about the Prince. The King and Queen met him, liked him, and gave their blessings on the marriage at once. The Prince and the Princess were married, and at the wedding feast all the guests played with the golden ball that had brought the Prince and Princess together.

Wiggly Giggles

I've got the wiggly-wiggles today,
And I just can't sit still.
My teacher says she'll have to find
A stop-me-wiggle pill.

I've got the giggly-giggles today;
I couldn't tell you why.
But if Mary hiccups one more time,
I'll giggle till I cry.

I've got to stamp my wiggles out
And hold my giggles in,
'Cause wiggling makes me giggle,
And gigglers never win.
Stacy Jo Crossen and Natalie Anne Covell

Crying

Crying only a little bit
is no use. You must cry
until your pillow is soaked!
Then you can get up and laugh.
Then you can jump in the shower
and splash-splash-splash!
Then you can throw open your window
and, "Ha ha! ha ha!"
And if people say, "Hey,
what's going on up there?"
"Ha ha!" sing back, "Happiness
was hiding in the last tear!
I wept it! Ha ha!"

Galway Kinnell

41

My Day

Merry Sunshine

"Good morning, Merry Sunshine,
How did you wake so soon,
You've scared the little stars away
And shined away the moon.
I saw you go to sleep last night
Before I ceased my playing;
How did you get way over there?
And where have you been staying?"

"I never go to sleep, dear child,
I just go round to see
My little children of the East,
Who rise and watch for me.
I waken all the birds and bees
And flowers on my way,
And now come back to see the child
Who stayed out late at play."

Anonymous

43

SPIKE GETS DRESSED

Each day I wake up
and I cuddle my bear.
Then I start to get dressed
in my white underwear.

What should I wear today?
What will I choose?
A blue shirt, some overalls,
some socks, and some shoes.

44

It's windy and frosty
and cold out today.
With my hat and my coat on,
I go out to play.

Can you point to where Kitty has been hiding?

45

Bad Day

by Gregory Maguire

Zachary loved surprises. Every morning, when the sun woke him, Zachary would sit up in his bed and play with his bear, Mr. Fuzzface, while he waited for Daddy or Mommy to awaken. He would talk with Mr. Fuzzface about the sort of surprises they might have during the day.

But one morning, Mr. Fuzzface wasn't there, and it was dark and cloudy outside. "What kind of surprise is that?" said Zachary. "Mr. Fuzzface, where are you? Daddy! Mommy! Where is Mr. Fuzzface?"

Mommy came in yawning and found Mr. Fuzzface on the floor. "You're awake an hour early," she said. "Can't you go back to sleep?"

Zachary wouldn't. Zachary *couldn't*. With Mr. Fuzzface dragging behind, Zachary headed for the kitchen.

Oh, no. Bad day. No more Crunchy Munchies for breakfast.

"It's not too bad," said Daddy. "You can have some toast for breakfast."

Zachary wouldn't. Zachary *couldn't*. But Mr. Fuzzface liked toast and jam, and turned all pink and sticky.

Oh, no. Terrible day. It was raining, so Zachary couldn't play in the yard.

"It really is terrible outside," said Mommy. "You can paint a picture instead. Why don't you do that?"

Zachary wouldn't. Zachary *couldn't*. He painted green cheeks and purple lips on Mr. Fuzzface instead.

Oh, no. Sad day. Because it was raining, Emily couldn't come over to play.

"Don't look so sad," said Mommy. "Why don't you make a little hat for Emily with your colored paper, and give it to her some other time?"

Zachary wouldn't. Zachary *couldn't*. He made a paper wig for Mr. Fuzzface instead, and taped his whiskers together.

Then Aunt Lola came over with a box. "This is something I'm giving to someone later," she said as she put the box on top of the refrigerator. "My, my! Mr. Fuzzface is looking a bit frazzled."

Zachary sent Mr. Fuzzface flying into space several times. Mr. Fuzzface was supposed to push the mysterious box off the refrigerator. But the bear landed next to the box and stayed there.

"Are you having a bad day?" asked Mommy.

"Mr. Fuzzface is in outer space," said Zachary.

"I think this would be a very good day for a surprise," said Aunt Lola.

"All the surprises today are bad ones," said Zachary.

"I'm going to bake a cake," said Mommy after she rescued Mr. Fuzzface from the refrigerator.

"Let me help, please?" asked Zachary.

"Why don't you make a cake with your modeling clay?" suggested Mommy.

Zachary wouldn't. Zachary *couldn't*. He made a yellow clay moustache and big blue clay eyebrows for Mr. Fuzzface instead.

The bad day was making Zachary tired, so Mommy put him to bed for a nap. Mr. Fuzzface looked a little strange, so Zachary pushed him out of bed. But then he missed his only bear, and cried himself to sleep. Crummy day! Bad, sad, lousy day! Day of no good surprises!

But when he woke up, the sun was out.

And Mr. Fuzzface didn't look scary in the sunlight. He looked *funny.*

And then the doorbell rang. Emily had arrived with five balloons, and Daddy was coming up the sidewalk with ice cream.

And Mommy said the ice cream would be perfect with her cake. The cake smells from the kitchen were so good that Mommy and Daddy decided to serve it right away.

So the bad day wasn't so bad anymore. And in the box on the refrigerator was another bear, a surprise from Aunt Lola.

"Would you like to introduce your new bear to Mr. Fuzzface?" asked Aunt Lola.

Zachary would. Zachary could. Zachary *did.*

And they all ate cake and ice cream, and the new bear fell in the ice cream only twice.

The Meal

Timothy Tompkins had turnips and tea.
The turnips were tiny.
He ate at least three.
And then, for dessert,
He had onions and ice.
He liked that so much
That he ordered it twice.
He had two cups of ketchup,
A prune, and a pickle.
"Delicious," said Timothy.
"Well worth a nickel."
He folded his napkin
And hastened to add,
"It's one of the loveliest breakfasts I've had."

Karla Kuskin

Advice

"Come along, come along,
　Don't take all day.
Hurry up, hurry up,"
　That's what they say.

"What are you doing
　With everyone gone,
Sitting and thinking,
　Your stocking half on?"

"Come along, come along,
　Don't be so slow."
That's what they tell me
　Wherever I go.

Marchette Chute

A Problem

My zipper is stuck
　And what shall I do?
Give it a jerk
　And break it in two,
Give it a tug
　And then it will jam—
I think I'll just sit here
　The way that I am.

Marchette Chute

As We Grow

I Wonder If I'm Growing

I wonder if I'm growing,
I wonder if I'm growing.
My Mum says yes, I'm growing,
But it's hard for me to see.

My Mum says, "Eat your sandwich,
It'll make you grow up tall,"
But when I eat my sandwich,
I'm hardly bigger at all.

My Mum says, "Wash your hands now,
Then you can go and play."
Hey, I can reach the tap now,
For the very first time today.

And I think I must be growing,
Yes I know I'm really growing.
My Mum says yes, I'm growing,
And now I know it's true.

Raffi

The Ugly Duckling

A Retelling of the Fairy Tale by Hans Christian Andersen

ne green and golden summer day, a mother duck sat on her nest by a quiet pond. She had been waiting for her eggs to hatch for a long time. But just as she thought she would never see her babies, the eggs began to crack. Soon, the proud mother duck was surrounded by five little ducklings. One egg was left.

Finally, the last and biggest egg hatched, and with a "Cheep! Cheep!" a big, fuzzy, gray baby bird tumbled out. "Oh!" said the mother duck. "What a strange-looking duckling! I don't think he could be my child. He's so ugly!"

The next day, the mother duck took her family swimming. Each duckling went into the water with a splash. "Quack, quack!" called the mother duck. "Follow me!" Then she noticed the ugly duckling gliding on the water. "What a good swimmer!" she thought. "But he doesn't swim like my other ducklings."

The ducks swam across the pond to a barnyard. When the barn-yard animals saw the mother duck and her new family, they said, "Look at that gray duckling. What an odd little fellow he is! We don't want him around here!" A chicken flew right at the ugly duckling and tried to peck at him.

"Leave him alone!" cried the mother duck. "He's not hurting anyone."

But the barnyard animals would not leave the ugly duckling alone. They teased him and snapped at him and pecked him all summer until he was so sad that he decided to run away. One day he crawled under the barnyard fence and started on his way to look for a new home.

Soon the duckling came to a pond full of ducks he did not know. He tried to play with them, but they swam away because he looked so different. The poor duckling was very lonely.

The winter months were coming, and all the ducks at the pond flew away. But the ugly duckling stayed because he had nowhere to go. One day he saw a flock of beautiful white birds flying over- head. They had lovely long necks. The ugly duckling had never seen such beautiful birds! He watched them until the last one dis- appeared. That winter, the poor duckling suffered terribly. One day the pond froze up all around him, and he was caught in the ice! He couldn't get out, so he slept in the icy pond all night.

The next morning, a farmer saw the duckling. He broke the ice and carried the duckling home to his family. The duckling quickly warmed up in the comfortable little house.

The children wanted to play with the duckling. But they were too rough with him, and the duckling fluttered away. In a panic, he flew into a pan of milk!

The children's mother screamed and waved her apron at the duckling, so he flew into the butter tub! Then, with the whole family chasing him, the duckling landed in the flour bin. He was covered with milk, butter, and flour as they chased him out of the house. The poor little duckling had to spend the rest of that terrible winter outside.

Spring came at last. The ugly duckling began to feel better as the days grew warmer. One day, he tried his wings, and he was able to fly. He flew until he came to a beautiful garden near a clear blue lake. On the lake were three white swans gliding lightly across the water with their elegant heads held high.

The duckling knew at once that the swans were the wonderful birds he had seen flying overhead last fall. He wanted to swim over to them and become their friend. "They would never be friends with an ugly duckling like me," he thought sadly. "But I will try anyway."

Shyly, the duckling glided onto the lake. The three swans swam toward him. The duckling was afraid. But then he saw his reflection in the water.

And what did he see there? A beautiful white swan! He wasn't an ugly duckling anymore. In fact, he had never been a duck at all. He had grown up to be a swan!

The three older swans circled around him and stroked him gently with their beaks. Some children playing at the edge of the lake threw bread to the birds. "Look!" they cried. "A new swan! And he is the prettiest of them all!"

The old swans bowed their heads in agreement. The duckling felt so shy that he tucked his head under his wing. But then his heart filled with joy, and he raised his long white neck. When he was an ugly duckling, he never dreamed he would be so happy.

ANNIE ASKS: WHAT MAKES ME GROW?

Will I get to be as tall as my mom and dad?
You probably will. You were created by two tiny cells – one from your mom and one from your dad. Each cell carries genes. Genes are like plans that carry all the information about what you will look like and how you will grow. Since your genes came from your parents, you'll probably grow to be as tall as they are. You may even be taller.

Why do baby teeth fall out?
Everybody has two sets of teeth. Your baby teeth are just the right size when you are small. As you grow, your baby teeth don't grow with you. New teeth develop under your baby teeth. The new, bigger teeth push the baby teeth out of the way, and the baby teeth fall out. The new teeth stay with you from then on.

Why do my nails grow?
Your nails grow to protect the tips of your fingers and toes. They grow from a nail root. Children's nails grow faster than grownups' nails. Nails grow fastest in hot weather.

Why doesn't it hurt when I get my hair cut?
The only parts of your hair that are alive and growing are the roots under your scalp. Your scalp is the skin on your head. When someone pulls your hair, it hurts because the roots are surrounded by nerves. Nerves sense pain. There are no nerves outside your head or in your hair. And, that's why you don't feel anything when strands of your hair are cut.

When will I stop growing?
Everyone grows at a different rate. If you are a girl, you'll probably stop growing around age 16. If you are a boy, you'll probably stop at age 18.

Birthdays

If birthdays happened once a week
Instead of once a year,
Think of all the gifts you'd get
And all the songs you'd hear
And think how quickly you'd
grow up;
Wouldn't it feel queer
If birthdays happened once a week
Instead of once a year?

Mary Ann Hoberman

The Wish

Each birthday wish
I've ever made
Really does come true.
Each year I wish
I'll grow some more
And every year
    I
      DO!

Ann Friday

Christy is having a surprise birthday party. All seven party guests are hiding. Can you find them?

Little People™ Big Book About OURSELVES

TIME-LIFE for CHILDREN™
Publisher: Robert H. Smith
Editorial Director: Neil Kagan
Associate Editor: Jean Burke Crawford
Marketing Director: Ruth P. Stevens
Promotion Director: Kathleen B. Tresnak
Associate Promotion Director: Jane B. Welihozkiy
Production Manager: Prudence G. Harris
Editorial Consultants: Jacqueline A. Ball, Sara Mark

FISHER-PRICE™
Director of Licensed Products: Edward P. Powderly
Marketing Manager, Licensed Products: Ronni Pollack
Product Approval Manager: Mary Ann Bittner
Licensing Administrator: Irwin J. Katzmann II

PRODUCED BY PARACHUTE PRESS, INC.
Editorial Director: Joan Waricha
Editors: Christopher Medina, Jane Stine, Ann Hardy,
    Wendy Wax
Writers: Lisa Eisenberg, Laura Hitchcock, Gregory Maguire,
    Natalie Standiford, Jean Waricha
Designer: Deborah Michel
Illustrators: Shirley Beckes, Molly Delaney, Ann Iosa,
    Rowan Barnes-Murphy, Daniel Sansouci,
    Karen Schmidt, John Spiers

ACKNOWLEDGMENTS

Every effort has been made to trace the ownership of all copyrighted material and to secure the necessary permissions. If any question arises as to the use of any material, the editor and the publisher, while expressing regret for any inadvertent error, will make the necessary correction in future printings.

Grateful acknowledgement is made to the following for permission to reprint the copyrighted material listed below: Addison-Wesley Publishing Co., Inc. for "Ears Hear" from OODLES OF NOODLES by Lucia M. and James L. Hymes, Jr. Copyright © 1964 by Lucia M. and James L. Hymes, Jr. Children's Better Health Institute, Benjamin Franklin Literary & Medical Society, Inc., Indianapolis, Indiana for "The Bear Who Wanted to Be a Bird" by Adele and Cateau de Leeuw, from CHILD LIFE. Copyright © 1947 by Child Life, Inc. E.P. Dutton, a division of Penguin Books USA Inc., for "Wiggly Giggles" from ME IS HOW I FEEL by Stacy Jo Crossen and Natalie Ann Covell. Copyright © 1970 by A. Harris Stone, Stacy Jo Crossen, Natalie Ann Covell, Victoria deLarrea; and "Sneezles" from NOW WE ARE SIX by A.A. Milne. Copyright © 1927 by E.P. Dutton and renewed 1955 by A.A. Milne. Harper & Row for "The Meal" from DOGS AND DRAGONS, TREES AND DREAMS: A COLLECTION OF POEMS BY KARLA KUSKIN. Originally published in ALEXANDER SOAMES: HIS POEMS. Copyright © 1962 by Karla Kuskin. Robert Luce Inc. for "Clap Your Hands" by Marion Grayson. Copyright © 1962 by Marion Grayson. Gina Maccoby Literary Agency for "Changing" and "Birthdays" by Mary Ann Hoberman. Copyright © 1981 by Mary Ann Hoberman. McClelland & Steward Ltd. for Canadian rights for "Sneezles" from NOW WE ARE SIX by A.A. Milne. Copyright © 1955 by A.A. Milne. Methuen Children's Books for United Kingdom rights for "Sneezles" from NOW WE ARE SIX by A.A. Milne. Copyright © 1955 by A.A. Milne. Houghton Mifflin for "Crying" from MORTAL ACTS, MORTAL WORDS by Galway Kinnell. Copyright © 1980 by Galway Kinnell. William Morrow & Co. for "Somersaults" from RAINY, RAINY SATURDAY by Jack Prelutsky. Copyright © 1980 by Jack Prelutsky. Random House for "Me I Am" from THE RANDOM HOUSE BOOK OF POETRY FOR CHILDREN by Jack Prelutsky. Copyright © 1983 by Random House Inc. Mary Chute Smith for "A Problem" and "Advice" from RHYMES ABOUT US by Marchette Chute. Coypright © 1974 by E.P. Dutton Inc. Troubadour Records for "I Wonder If I'm Growing." Words by Raffi, D. Pike, B&B Simpson. Copyright © 1976 by Homeland Publishing, a division of Troubadour Records.

Library of Congress Cataloging-in-Publication Data

Little people big book about ourselves.
    p. cm.—(Little people big books)
    Summary: A collection of original stories, classic fairy tales, non-fiction pieces, poems, activities, and games.
    ISBN 0-8094-7458-1.—ISBN 0-8094-7459-X (lib. bdg.)
    1. Children's literature. [1. Literature—Collections.] I. Time-Life for Children (Firm)   II. Title: About ourselves.
    III. Series.
PZ5.L7258   1989   89-5232
                                                                                     CIP
                                                                                     AC

TIME-LIFE BOOKS
ALEXANDRIA, VIRGINIA

Things I Can Do

There are many things I can do
Maybe you can do them too;

I know how to climb a tree
I can even buzz like a bee,
I can also wash my face
And I know how to run a race.
I know how to talk to a dog
I can even croak like a frog,
I can also sail a boat
And I know how to sink not float.

I know how to build a house
I can even be still as a mouse,
I can also kick a ball
And I know how to never fall.

I know how to tame a bear
I can even comb my hair,
I can also catch a snake
And I know how to stay awake.

There are many more things I can do
Tomorrow I'll teach them all to you.

B. Taylor Bradford